Grief:

Process of Healing

Moonsoulchild

Grief: Process of Healing

Grief: Process of Healing

Copyright © 2020 Sara Sheehan
All Rights Reserved
ISBN: 9798629161318

Grief: Process of Healing

Grief: Process of Healing

Welcome to my healing process.

Please, note this is from my experiences and I can't make or truly heal your own being. I'm not a therapist. If what I provide doesn't help, I'm sorry. Grief is a tough pill to swallow. It's something we forever hold with us. Losing a loved one is never easy. Whether it was someone who's no longer in your life but still out there in the world, or someone who passed on. Death is hard to understand. Death is not an easy topic to sit and discuss because it's so terrifying. I'm currently at a place in my life where I understand, not saying I can accept what fate has placed in front of me when it comes to being without someone I love. I learned to use certain ways to cope. The process isn't easy, you need to have an open mind and heart. You need to be ready to face the emotions you're feeling at every waking moment. Grieving is scary, it's sometimes forever. I'm here to help you understand. I'm here to help ease the pain. I'm here to show you what you think you lost, is still very real. I hope this collection brings you peace. I hope it brings a new perspective.

Grief: Process of Healing

To think people, pass on, it's a lot to grasp. People we love, it seems impossible. Every day I wake up alive is a blessing I don't take for granted.

I saw death in many ways, the slow, you know it's coming and the unexpected. They both are heart wrenching.

I gained a new perspective on how to heal from a loss. Even though it's excruciating, there's a way through. Death is makes life unbearable to get through. You feel lost with no direction. Complete utter sadness. A shattered heart that won't ever be healed. It forever holds the same pain every time you relive that memory. The difference now, I don't hold pain that pain every day. It's not constant. I laugh, smile, and continue to love.

Losing someone I love that can't be physically near, it's hard to accept. To never get to call or text, to get to experience life with them, it hurts. It takes a while to realize it's going to be your reality.

Once you accept what fate has for your loved one, you will start seeing the signs they never left. Their soul is more alive than ever and protects and guides you every day.

Angel numbers (333) any consistency of numbers in a sequence. The moon. Butterflies. Birthdays. Stars.

Grief: Process of Healing

All of those always remind me of my loved ones. Just the simple things they loved bring me comfort.

When you see a sign, speak to them. They're always there, they just need you to ask for help and they will make it happen. They don't want you to be dwelling in their absence.

I have beautiful spirits protecting me.

The power of a soul when it's invisible, is something I find so beautiful yet heartbreaking. To think I'll never hear their laugh, or see their face, it used to bring me to a dark place. Now, I'm keeping myself together for their sake. At times I feel most vulnerable, they're there to remind me I'm not alone.

A message to my angels,

Even though I cry every time I think of you, it doesn't mean I'm sad, it means I'm feeling you.

Grief: Process of Healing

Death is one of the hardest things to accept, and to move on from. The person you love is no longer in human form. It's something all of us will never completely understand because our hearts take over and our minds are clouded by the heart break to think clearly. It's something we beat ourselves up about because we can't balance love and loss.

We can't accept someone's road ended and we're supposed to keep going. It's a painful experience.

But listen,

When that someone loved you as much as you loved them, you will feel their spirit live on. You will feel the love every day with little reminders you're not alone.

But first,

You will live in pain searching for the answers until you realize there's no answer. Life doesn't make sense, and it's not up to us to analyze it.

So, promise me you won't try to understand and spend more time living.

Grief: Process of Healing

There are two types of grief,

The heart wrenching loss of someone who can't every be physically present again, only in spirit.

Then,

The loss of someone you loved for so long who's out there in the world with no trace of how they're doing.

        They both hurt the heart.

Grief: Process of Healing

Losing someone who is still alive hurts just as much as death. You invested a lot of time and love into this human. You grew to be a part of their life. The power of the human heart is breathtaking. It allows you to still love even after the person wronged you, or you wronged them. The power of love is unexplainable, I believe it doesn't need to be spoken, it's felt.

Grieving someone who you can't contact or wants nothing to do with you is confusing. I believe it hurts the heart a bit more knowing they're out there in the world and you can't know a thing about them.

You need to understand,

You're not obligated to know. Once that tie you once had with this person is cut, you have no right to know about their growth. It's a life lesson that needs to be taught. I only wish I was told this.

Latching onto what was once there and convincing yourself you can get it back when it's came to an end. Stop finding ways to recover the loss, love what's bloomed. I know it's hard to see through the pain. I know it's not easy to accept a loss that wasn't your choice but continuing to fight for someone who doesn't fight back will only damage you.

Grief: Process of Healing

You won't be for everyone and everyone won't be for you. Just because you shared a moment in time, or many, doesn't mean you are forever embedded in their life. Nothing in life is permanent, I mean, look at all of us, we all pass on when our time comes.

Stop holding onto what's no longer serving you purpose. Stop holding onto what's holding you back. You will stunt your growth every time you try to get something back that found its way out.

>Understand this,

>Make peace with it and move on.

Write a letter to someone you lost that's still out there:

_____

_____

_____

_____

_____

_____

Grief: Process of Healing

Grief: Process of Healing

"It's a part of life,

Losing people and realizing the friends you had aren't meant to grow with you.

It's not the end,

You just to remember
you don't need a single soul to live."

Grief: Process of Healing

"Sometimes we need to hurt to understand it's not what's for us.

Sometimes we're stubborn and choose not to go down a road of destruction knowing it will only bring us pain without realizing it will bring us through."

Grief: Process of Healing

"I'm sorry my soul
Won't ever get to rest without you.
I'm sorry I always saw the soulmate in you.
I'm sorry I loved you
Even when you didn't deserve it.
I'm sorry I still do."

Grief: Process of Healing

"We all make it through. I thought I was broken. Damaged, lost, not whole, but never broken.

Every day is another day to keep going,
The hurt you feel may last awhile but the longer you dwell in the pain and the loss, the longer it will hurt.

Everyone experiences pain differently,
We all feel different,
One thing for sure,
We all heal,
It's up to you to let yourself."

Grief: Process of Healing

2017 I lost control,
I lost sight of everything that mattered.
My mind was a dark place,
My heart, I couldn't feel the beat.
It felt like I was living but I wasn't alive,
I survived.
Every day I felt myself die a little inside.
I didn't know how to recover,
I didn't know how to undo the pain.
I wanted it to be over,
I wanted to feel happiness.
I lost control of myself,
I let myself fall deeper into my head.
Even with people around I loved,
Once we departed and I was alone
Everything I felt turned upside down.
Their presence was temporary bliss,
A quick pick me up
Until I was alone and could think.
My mind always was my worst enemy,
It overplayed memories,
Happy ones
Death of loved ones held weight on me.
I couldn't express because no one felt,
I was grieving a loss on my own.
I grieved in silence,

Grief: Process of Healing

I cried until there wasn't any more tears,
I asked God why, many times
I tried to analyze the situation
I studied memories,
I made myself feel the loss, for once,
I soaked in the pain.
I let the universe bring me through.
I overcame my depression,
The moment I chose to acknowledge it
The best decision I could have made.

After years of running from pain,
I chose to understand it,
I chose to feel it regardless how it ended.
I found beauty in it.

Depression doesn't control me anymore,
I learned to control it,
I learned to let it drift off slow,
I didn't need it overstaying it's welcome.
I made peace with that feeling,
I grew from it once I utterly understood it.

I now have a better understanding,
Not everything came to kill me,
It came to give me strength,
It came to help me understand
Why I loved in the first place.

Grief: Process of Healing

I would like to take you down a very personal healing journey, mine.

In the next pages I will share letters I wrote to a dear friend of mine, whom I lost three years ago. She lost her life to Asthma. I won't give too much of a back story, I would like you to hear my story through these letters. Every letter I wrote at a time I needed her to hear me. I needed to release every emotion stemming through my heart. I saw a way to talk to her.

Giving advice about grief isn't easy because we all grieve differently. There's no right or wrong way. I believe the best way to get guidance on grieving is to see inside someone's healing process and seeing there's light at the end of it all.

I hope these letters bring you some peace,
They saved my life.

"Young Naked Soul"

If I asked anyone to explain what "Young Naked Soul" meant, they would probably refer it to someone being young and naked, and forget the most important part, soul. When I hear those three words, I think about you, Josie. Someone who was young and had a naked mindset, one not many understood. A mindset which had no limits, you did whatever set your soul on fire. You lived true to you and the truth of your own life. Naked doesn't always mean being without clothes, anyone can be naked. To share your spirit, fears, deepest thoughts, and feelings with someone, that's being naked. You give someone the power to destroy you, with hopes they don't break you. Who would have thought those three words would hold so much meaning?

I can't accept the fact this nightmare haunts me every day. I don't know how to feel. I don't know what to do. I know you would want me to enjoy my life and be happy, but it's so hard being happy when you're broken. You took a part of me I'll never receive back. I've never felt this kind of heartbreak.

Grief: Process of Healing

While having many people I love, your piece overpowers them all. They say it hurts more when you miss someone you can't have while they're alive, knowing there's room for a fix. Missing someone who isn't every coming back? Like impossible? That's true heart break. Knowing there's nothing I can do to bring you back breaks me. Thinking of every little thing I've gotten mad about makes me feel horrible. So many emotions played into so many different things that I will tell you soon, as you already know. I know you knew I loved you, but did you know I completely adored you? When I first met you, my first thought was "she's the most beautiful woman I've ever seen" now, you're gone.

Sometimes it's hard to breathe.
Sometimes it's hard to keep the tears in.
Sometimes it's hard to believe it's real.

I look at your social media about once a day, staring at your pictures because they're all that's left of you. Hoping you'll text me you miss me. This is a horrible nightmare. I'm hurting. All I can do is live off our memories together.

I am so thankful to have known you. You changed my outlook on everything in life.

Grief: Process of Healing

Before and now. You made me realize life is too short to hold things in. To always tell the ones you love, you love them. You showed me what it's like to be yourself. You taught me by accepting me for everything I am.

You lived a beautiful life and had amazing people in your corner whom I didn't get to meet until after you're gone. I'm so happy to witness them speak on you. They said everything I already knew. You were perfect in your own way. You never expressed your entire being to me, you always held back a bit. I understand now, I'm just having a hard time accepting that I understand.

Someone who can live every day like it's their last, while keeping a positive mindset is the most amazing thing I've ever witnessed. You had your bad times, but you always made the good outweigh them. You were always so strong. I admired a lot about you.

You were the one person to spend my birthday with me last year. You came an hour away to see me and it was eventful. Some may say it could have been better, but I'd take night on the beach watching you fight about whether it was a shooting star or a plane in the sky. Taking pointless selfies and watching the beach with you, one more time all over again. I'm going to a concert at the end of this month and I'm overwhelmed because that's the last place I saw you. Even though I hated how the night started, it was pouring, and my outfit was ruined. You surprised me by showing up, the rain stopped, and the night became everything. But that night was the last time I saw you, so it's kind of bittersweet. To have such mixed emotions about one night, I'm just struggling a bit.

    I want to thank you for giving me some of my greatest memories. Thank you so much for blessing my life with your existence. I will forever remember ever single memory you've given me. I might not have been close to you to the point I knew every dimension of you, we didn't get much time. But you showed me everything I needed to know.

    I'm learning to deal with this, I'm trying hard Josie. My heart has never been broken, but I don't know how to stop analyzing why God chose you. I'm trying to accept the fact you're now my guardian angel. I'm trying hard to not break down when your soul was so pure. You touched everyone who loved you. I've become numb to everything. You told me on June 22, 2016: "I will never leave you, I promise", but you're gone, and I know this wasn't your plan, you would have never left me. I don't blame God for wanting you, I am mad at him. I'm angry he chose to take someone so special to many of us, someone who was different and showed it. Someone who wasn't afraid to live. Someone who touched so many souls. Someone who stayed true to herself. Why did he take you? The one person who was good. You didn't deserve this, but he has better plans for you.

I will forever be mending in hopes to see you again and for my broken heart to be healed. I won't forget your smile, or you talk my ear off the whole car ride home. I miss you very much and that won't ever change.

So yes,

Those three words will always remind me of you,

Young Naked Soul

Those three words mean more to me than they will anyone I try and explain them to. Your life may be over, but who you were, your soul, will forever life on.

I love you Josephine.

Grief: Process of Healing

July 13, 2017

To the gorgeous, most breathtaking human I've ever laid my eyes on. This is for you Josephine. It's been two months since you got called home. What is life without you? I dread thinking about the number 17 when it comes up on my calendar. Knowing you're gone another month, to think it will become years. It seems so impossible to cope. My heart hurts for the love I never got to express to you. My heart hurts because your life was just starting, and you have life still here and it's beautiful. You left behind so much beautiful. To think of you not being able to experience that beautiful anymore breaks me. I don't know if I could get passed that.

I'm blessed to have someone like you watching over me. I'm happy to have you. But I will forever be heartbroken and wish you were here, whole and not in spirit. I know that time heals all wounds, but these are too deep to heal.

Life is precious, but it's also short so you need to live everyday like you won't live another. You need to live like you're not afraid of too lose it all. You knew you loved with everything you had and that you'd leave parts of you with the ones you loved. How could I forget you?

You created the meaning to Young Naked Soul, a beautiful name you chose. You loved your life. You let many of us love you. I miss you, and love you, so much. My heart goes out to your family, I can't imagine the pain they're going through. I wish them all the love, healing and prayers possible. My heart goes out to your friends, and the ones who meant everything to you, they lost apart of them they'll never be able to move on from.

Through all the sadness,
Through the positive you see so much people who love you, and they realize you're never really gone. You're here. Having a piece of you is endless.

There's no one I could ever meet who will be half as beautiful as you. No one will ever make me want to life differently. You are a vibrant soul. Still, forever, always. I'm so glad God let your soul stop by, wouldn't have wanted it any other way.

Rest easy, love.
Remember,
No one can replace you, Young Naked Soul.

August 30, 2017

It's August 30, 2017 at 10:38 p.m. to be exact. The last time I really wrote was May 1, 2017. I couldn't seem to find the words, even one thought to make a whole feeling. I'm feeling you a little extra today. I've started this thing where I'm writing for you. I know you hear me. I know you're smiling down at me, telling me, keep being amazing. I couldn't be happier to have someone like you watching over me. I feel, well, you. I feel you so deeply. It feels as if you're right next to me. A high I don't ever want to come down from. Which is crazy because I also feel broken. I also feel like I won't ever get by, like I won't ever understand why you had to be taken so soon. I will never understand what I completely feel because I can't feel you. I feel like everything that once was there, has gone with you. It's like I'm lost and trying so hard to find it. That feeling is so powerful yet heartbreaking.

Grief: Process of Healing

I never understood death. I could never cope with it. I had a habit of pushing things behind me to deal with the pain. Sometimes we change for the better. Sometimes we change according to situations, and sometimes, we don't change for the better. I taught myself how to not feel. When my grandparents passed, I was a wreck. I was so wrecked I put it in the back of my mind because I thought not feeling it would help me cope with it. To this day, when I think of them, I just have tears. I didn't let myself feel it. I didn't understand what death meant. I couldn't grasp the thought of losing someone forever. I didn't understand being able to feel was important. I taught myself how to not feel, to not understand the importance of a heart. I was heartless but my heart was always there under the darkness. Sometimes you go through something and never come out the same. Sometimes pain changes you for the worst if you let it.

When I met you, I didn't know what I was in for, or why we crossed paths. I always analyze every moment and replaying memories because I want to remember and relive every single moment over and love, like it just happened. I don't ever want too to forget what you meant to me. What I wish I could have told you, that's why I hope you're listening. I hope you can hear me right now. Sometimes I think, is it normal to try and analyze every moment? Am I crazy? Because I can still imagine your smile, the exact image in my head is so real. I can feel it. I've never appreciated your facial expressions as much I do now, other than your smile, I felt that the moment I met you. You sparked something in me, as I wish I would have taken the request. You showed me I was missing the most important thing ever, the power to feel. I hid because I was afraid to love you. I learned what it felt like to no longer be whole. I learned what it felt like, to have your heart ripped out your chest and slammed back in. because well, people with good hearts always come out strong. That's what you taught me. You showed me how much a person could feel that there's no limit. The more you feel the stronger you become. I no longer care when people tell me to stop being emotional, stop being sad. Being sad is a part of feeling, how can you be happy without knowing what it's like to feel weakness? I wish you didn't have to leave. I wish this was all a horrible nightmare. I will never understand a lot of things, but I'm sure of one thing, being able to feel is the greatest gift you gave me, other than your unconditional love.

Sometimes I drown in the thought of being without you. Sometimes I feel like you're not gone. Sometimes I'm selfish because I can't have you whole. I just don't get it. I know I need to accept it. I need to understand what's real. You're in spirit, in soul, not in whole. To me, you'll always be whole. You'll always be soul, my Young Naked Soul.

The greatest friend who has ever blessed me with the greatest lesson of life. Showing me what it's like to be myself completely. Not being afraid to feel. To love deeply, always. You will always be the first woman I ever loved, just by your smile.
Just by being you.

Grief: Process of Healing

October 5, 2017

You've been heavy on my heart lately, never once left my mind. I always think of you and I smile, I cry. Sometimes I'm confused. The feeling is overwhelming beautiful. It's like as heartbroken I feel, you make it feel like you never left. Your face implanted in my brain is what gets me through most days. Five months ago, I lived through one of the hardest things I've ever experienced. Five months ago, I didn't think I would be as strong as I am today. Even as an angel, your soul sets every friend in my life to shame.

I will forever celebrate your soul.
Just like you told me you'd never leave me,
Thanks for reminding me.
I love you.

Grief: Process of Healing

November 17, 2017

There's something incredibly special in knowing I have the best guardian angel. But also, very heartbreaking. Today marks 7 months since you've been gone. And it still feels like a horrible nightmare.

There are days I'll think of you like you're still here, not "forgetting" you're gone, but the fact it's still so unreal. I scroll through your twitter and see your last tweet and I think why she hasn't tweeted in so long!

I feel crazy because I still feel like you're here. Like you're one call away, but then reality hits and you can't be reached. I can't just see you smile or hear your laugh, but I can watch every video and replay that exact moment, every time and it all becomes surreal. My heart breaks every time.

I have days where I will talk to you for hours, whether I write or have a whole cry season asking God to please let me feel you one last time, to let you let me know you're okay.

Grief: Process of Healing

But you've been showing me signs since you left. You've been reaching out to me every day in the simplest ways that people will call me crazy for. But it's so comforting knowing it's you.

You promised you'd never leave, and you kept that promise. Breaks my heart. Like I love you so much and I miss you terribly. I wish I knew how I could be the greatest friend to you when you're already the greatest.

Even though this day makes me so sad it brings me to an understanding of how to live without you in life, but that I'll always have you in spirit.

I'm so blessed.
I will always celebrate you.

Grief: Process of Healing

April 17, 2018

I've been dreading this day since last year. I can feel every emotion I was left with when I knew you were gone. I still remember the pain I felt when a piece of me left with you. The heartache I had; I will forever feel that heartache.

I published my first poetry book in your honor, to celebrate your life with a dedication to you. I took something positive and made it reality because I know you'd want me happy today, not drowning in my sorrows.

There's no amount of time that will pass that will make my heart hurt less, there's nothing that can make my heart not yearn for your love. I'm still broken. I feel you tremendously today, and as this is supposed to be my happiest moment, we should be celebrating this moment, but I've had my moment and I will live on to keep living in that moment. But right now, this moment, is yours.

This moment, I faced a year of heart break, confusion and depression. I faced a whole year without you, and I didn't think I could live

Grief: Process of Healing

through that, but your signs showed me how important it was to be strong for you.
You never left anything go unnoticed, you always showed up for me, you supported me through everything I believed in, and even after you're gone, you've made this journey one of my most meaningful journeys. I couldn't have gotten here without your help, I feel all of you, so intensely, you showed up, you made sure I made this happen.

Loving you, Josie, was one of the best decisions I've made. It was you, who helped me understand me, and to not accept less than I give. I pray to God you're always looking over me, because there's no energy I want around me, other than the most comforting energy you give me, I am most thankful for that. I'm thankful that even though I can't help you, that I can't bring you back, you still always show up for me.

You are the definition of a forever friend and I can't thank you enough for showing me that. I hope I made you proud, I hope you know I'm broken but I'm mending because of you.

Nothing will ever be forgotten about you, your soul is too beautiful to ever be forgotten.
I love you so much.

Grief: Process of Healing

July 13, 2018 12:34 a.m.

I want to start by saying, thank you Josie. Thank you for being the most amazing angel I could've asked for, and though that's the last thing I ever wanted. I've never felt as safe as I do now that I have you by my side. This year has been an experience at the least.

I've done things out of my comfort zone and I believe it's because I've had you by my side, guiding me into the right direction. You always knew what was best, you were the best. You still are. I hope heaven is as beautiful as you, God is lucky to have you. He's lucky to have someone as wonderful as you.

I miss you endlessly. The memories I'll always have save me from completely losing it. Seeing your face on my phone every time I look at my wallpaper. The love I have for you will never be forgotten. You've given me some of my greatest life moments. You've given me the greatest love I've ever could've received, so pure, so honest.

Grief: Process of Healing

It's so hard to capture everything that has happened, and to believe you're truly gone. It all still feels like a terrible nightmare. You've helped me see the light at the end of the road. You've helped me mend my broken heart, even though a piece has left with you. That piece will remain gone, and I will always feel empty when it comes to that piece, until I see you again.

Your soul is forever alive, and beautiful Josephine. It's too beautiful to be forgotten. You're too beautiful to ever be forgotten. I can't thank you enough for still being wonderful and being the greatest soul mate.

I'm wishing you a happy birthday my love. I hope you're doing great up there; I miss you dearly here. I know you're here. I know you're with us all today. We're going to celebrate your beautiful soul. This one's for you.

Happy 26th birthday Josephine, rock the heavens. I love you, till we meet again, I'll always search for you within the moon,
I know I'll find you there.

Grief: Process of Healing

August 27, 2018 10:30 p.m.

It's been so long. I haven't had this kind of release for over a year, the kind where I lay my heart out to you because I know you're near, and I know you hear.

Josephine, I miss you so much. Sometimes I stop and think to myself and remember your peaceful smile that brought me the kind of joy I search for within friends I've lost in hopes I could fill the void of you. I try to make friends to fill the void you've taken with you, but no one has ever made me comfortable enough to give my most intimate thoughts, my deepest secrets, are all with you. I've never felt as safe I do, other than when you're in my presence, and with you not being here, your spirit is more alive than you could believe.

I feel you, very deeply at this moment and I wish I could just give you a hug and thank you for being the greatest, most amazing friend I've ever chose to let in. I wish I could see you one last time to tell you how much I'm truly thankful for all the light you've brought into my life after all the tragedy. Everything that I've been through in the past months haven't felt as bad with you by my side guiding me to the part of my life I needed to be. I prayed you were here to see me grow. I prayed you were here to see all my accomplishments, and to see where I'm going next.

I've found true happiness, and that's all because I had the greatest guardian angel guiding me to the light. I couldn't have done this without you, your signs, your energy, has gotten me to accept my flaws because we both know how hard it is to overcome them and loving yourself is a challenge. But you, you've helped me see the importance of self-love, and how amazing it is to be fearless when it comes to loving yourself.

How beautiful it feels, to be free. I've become the free spirit I am, with the help of you. Your friendship has saved the parts of me I thought I lost years ago; your friendship saved my sanity. Of course, there's never a day that passes when I ask God if it's possible to see you one last time, but I know we'll meet again, not under these circumstances. I've come to accepting I have you

in spirit, and even though you're not whole,
you're whole in spirit and you're always here.

You don't miss a moment. I feel you; I find parts
of you everywhere. Your soul is the most alive,
and still as powerful and beautiful as I
remembered. You've guided me to my
happiness, you never failed me.

I've been trying to accept what fate had instore
for you. I've tried to understand why you're
gone, but I always come up short. But I've been
trying to analyze less, and be thankful more,
that I have you, and your friendship is what
keeps my soul alive.

Grief: Process of Healing

July 13, 2019

I remember being lost without you, somedays it felt hard to start my day, then some days I was distracted until it became time to rest, and my mind would go to the darkest place. I remember trying to find answers to something that didn't have one. I cried a lot. I was anxious every day. I felt like I was living on the edge and my emotions just took me by surprise.

A whole year of being lost because death was something I never understood, and feeling the loss was never something I let myself be open to, until you came and made me feel every feeling I felt losing you.

Today, my heart is healed. I'm no longer broken, I mended, because of you. I felt every emotion that came along with grieving and coming to terms with your soul living on, but also being put to rest. It was a weird balance of trying to heal and not becoming a mess.

Somedays I find myself reminiscing about our memories and sob, and others I'm thankful to have your guidance.

Grief: Process of Healing

What I learned, was regardless how long it's been or whether I'm healed, it's still possible to be strong and still miss you.

It's healthy to still cry.
It's healthy to keep your soul alive.

It doesn't matter if it was just yesterday, or 20 years from now, my heart will always be uneasy when it comes down to you. It always misses you. The heartache won't ever disappear, someone like you won't ever be forgotten.

You walked in and left the biggest imprint on my heart, and you reached my soul. I can't thank you enough, for everything you do to keep the light shining on me and guiding me to the road of my happiness.

I thank God always, for bringing you into my life, and getting the gift to be someone you loved. No one's soul can match yours, Josie. No one's love can replace the piece of my heart you took with you, it will always be with you and because of that, I'm a peace.

Happy birthday, Josie, I love you so much.

October 8, 2019

I remember feeling broken many times after break ups, mainly because I chose to give more than I demanded in return, so that resulted in my own heart break. I was never broken. I was just lost. I know now, I never experienced real heart break until the day I lost you.

The heartbreak of losing you gave me a rush of anxiety, and complete utter sadness that I didn't think I could ever come back from. I wanted you near, I wanted you in whole. I wanted you to be with your family, your daughter, and everyone who loves you. I was heartbroken for their souls too, to know how I felt losing you, I could only imagine the pain they also endured, so my heart is broken for them too.

Grief: Process of Healing

I remember crying and trying to find answers without understanding I wasn't going to find one, because there wasn't one. I felt alone trying to heal from the heartache, as I struggled to get through with just my writing because that's how I spoke to you, or finding myself under the moon because that's where I always felt you.

I spent a whole year trying to grieve in the darkness of people telling me "I'm sorry you lost her, but I can be your friend" in better words, people who didn't understand how it felt to have your heart ripped out your chest and not yet reached its destination back. I found it cruel that no one understood my pain, as it was written all over me. I felt the pain everyday as I tried desperately to hide behind the smile I gave off, I became real good at pretending, that by night, I found myself alone and just bursting into tears trying to understand how it was all possible. I tried analyzing many times, I tried to make sense of it all, but all that repeated was the memories of the times I spent my happiest times with you, to only being able to look back at those moments without creating more.

Grief: Process of Healing

I am heart broken by the loss of you, there's still the piece you took with you. I lived a whole year lost without direction, a whole year of trying to understand the vacant part of my soul that needed your presence. April 17, 2019 will be 2 years since you left, and 1 year since my book released in your honor, and I'm so proud, as I hope you are too, of my accomplishments, and for my broken heart I mended, the piece you took, realizing it's possible to go on without that piece, because I don't need that piece, it's yours.

I no longer like the term "I'm sorry for your loss" because your spirit and soul is still so rare and still very alive, I feel you everywhere I go, within different parts of my day, you make sure to let me know you never really left me. It was a long road of being confused without knowing it was possible to come back from this, I prayed a lot to have you back.

Instead,

I got waking up every morning at 3 a.m. with the moon shining through my window, a cute little blue orb under the moon in all my pictures, and how you brought the love of my life to me at the time I needed it most. The inspiration of finding myself through all the madness, everything that transitioned after your passing was dull until you came and brought all the light I needed.

To have a guardian angel as beautiful as you, I'm blessed, and incredibly thankful to have known you, to have loved you, to have felt you, as I continue to hold you close to my heart.

I don't search for friends no longer, I don't search for anything unless it's within myself, to make myself the best version of me, you taught me how important that is.

I will forever be living to prove the inspiration you flowed through me will always be alive.
You will always be a part of me, Josie.
We are one now, and forever.
I miss you dearly, but I'm so happy you're near.
Thank you for showing me what a real friendship is.

Grief: Process of Healing

January 1, 2020

Josie,

I can't forget the pain I feel when it comes to remembering the loss of you. I can't forget the depression I was stuck in trying to make sense of your passing. I cried endless tears. I did everything I could to feel close to you again. I reminisced memories of us. I thought of my favorite moments, only to be sunk deeper into my anxious nerves. I was forced to understand death. I was forced to feel. I couldn't comprehend why you were placed into my life just to pass through so soon. I tried to put pieces together that didn't fit, just to find an answer.

I prayed every night to get a sign from you. I pray every night to somehow heal from the pain of losing you. I felt alone as no one around me knew you, the ones who did, didn't feel you like I did. I had people tell me they'd be my friend, as if that would make me hurt less.

I went to therapy. I talked about you to someone I didn't know, as if it could help me heal, I thought maybe they could bring some insight on what I felt I was missing.

As time went on, I lost connections with people who I loved for almost decades, to people I loved for years. The signs started presenting, they weren't hard to notice, they were so clear.

I remember every little sign.

I remember every feeling I've felt when you presented your soul to me in spirit form.

I remember praying for you to come back. I remember being helpless, not thinking I would ever make it through.

I remember wishing it was all a nightmare, and I'd wake up and you'd be here.

I didn't think it was possible, the number of tears I cried. I didn't think it was possible, the amount of loneliness I felt, grieving over you without the shoulder of anyone that could remotely feel me.

It was a rollercoaster of emotions you left me with. I succumbed every battle I thought I'd lose, I made it through, with the help of you. Loneliness felt less once you touched my soul.

Grief: Process of Healing

To wish to have you back, but to be in touch with your afterlife soul, a beautiful miracle I've witnessed. You have brought the brightest light into my life, while taking out the darkest parts that kept me down. My life has little mishaps since you've been my angel, everything is aligning how you knew I deserved. I know it's all because of you, it's been nothing but miracles since you've made sense of your departure.

I was once bitter, angry, and confused. You brought my life a new sense of understanding and purpose. I no longer look at death and see sadness, I know it's going to hurt, it's going to take time, but what I'll always remember, is no matter what you showed me while living, you also showed me afterlife.

Your soul keeps shining. My beautiful moon, I always search for you in the night, as you shine bright through my window. I didn't know what a true friend was until I met you, because the most important lessons in life you taught me, to love and let go, and even when letting go, you can still love.

I miss you so much.

Grief: Process of Healing

January 13, 2020

The biggest loss I felt, to the biggest gain. A feeling of both lost and blessed, an unknown emotion humanly possible, some might say it's a rollercoaster of a confusing mess, but I, call it the cost of loving you.

Losing you was the moment I realized what I was facing in life. I gained perspective on the ugliness and the beauty of it; growing connections, to loving, to completely breaking.

Life is about feeling, about moments. Moments that could be the rest of your life, or become a memory, always keep the love alive, but learn to detach from the idea it will ever exist in the same form it was first felt. Growing connections is a raw experience, something that only be felt. Soulmates meant to align with you, some you forced, know they don't always stay.

Life taught me to never stop giving my heart, even if it wasn't meant to be felt. To never give up on love because I chased for the wrong ones, at the wrong times, for the wrong reasons.

Grief: Process of Healing

Never let myself turn cold because I refuse to feel, to heal, to let myself be loved or to love again.

Never quit on myself when it comes to being broken, to build myself back up and to go harder. To humble myself, and know I have a heart that can't be matched, but someone will feel it the way needed.

I've seen the darkness; I've seen the light. I let go of loved ones, for myself. I was put in the crossfire, at many crossroads, searching for a new road to self. Went through many changes, grieving and being guided by you. Lost what I never thought I'd survive without, to finding what I never thought I needed, learning to love you in spirit. I made life worth living, finding happiness within myself, to opening doors to happiness within other souls.

I found my way, searching to find ways to make you whole again. I found strength in the cards I was dealt, when I accepted your soul will always be alive, but that doesn't stop me from ever missing you.

Grief: Process of Healing

April 17, 2020

It's easy to fall into a slump of the thought of you being gone. It's easy to cry when I suddenly think of you. What's not easy, is trying to hold myself together even after all these years.

It's been 3 years since you got called home and I've been here trying to make peace with your absence. My grieving journey has been long, my heart never rests when you come to mind. You're never forgotten, and you've made sure it wasn't an option. Your death hit my soul in such a dark way, I was faced to grieve alone until I connected and friended ones close to you.

I was so lost and confused, having to be upfront with what I was feeling and accepting the fate you've been given, and myself, was one of the hardest things I had to live through. There're no words to explain the pain my heart felt, or the scar on my soul that will forever be open because I refuse to let you go.

A connection we had that blossomed as soon as we met, the friend I needed all those years I went without. I analyzed why I felt so lifeless, I couldn't imagine my pain even touching the amount of those who knew you for years, or life, but truthfully, there's no amount of time that could make me love you more than I already do, that's why I believe our souls are tied.

    I wished I knew you longer and the friendship that could have grown wouldn't have ended before it began, the hardest thing to make peace with. I have sunk in a deep depression alone without the outside world knowing, but you, you dragged me into healing. You helped guide me into a new life, one that brings so much love and happiness. I only wish it didn't take losing you to find myself, I only wish I could have you along the side of me.

    3 years ago, I wouldn't have believed I would be where I am today, I never thought I've recovered from the tragedy of losing you. Here I am, 3 years later, not without you, but with you stronger than ever. Your soul is the most magical, peaceful, comforting soul I've ever witnessed. Thank you for never forgetting me, for keeping me safe. I feel you every day, a piece of you is forever embedded within me. I'll continue to look for you whenever the moon is out, I'll forever be missing you.

"I knew I was special
To be loved by you"

Grief: Process of Healing

I hope when you read those letters, you felt my heartache. There's something about re-reading these myself that bring me closer to healing. My heart has never been broken until the day I lost her. It's mending every day. As the days go by, I don't ever forget her. She keeps me on my feet with her daily reminders. I feel her.

I think the most important thing to try and find something that makes you feel closer to them. Whether it's a material item, text messages, pictures. It's immensely helpful to hold close.

Memories can be temporary,
The way you feel is forever.

Grief: Process of Healing

Someone once said to me,
"It's annoying when someone posts so many
pictures, instead of enjoying the moment."

I couldn't match that energy,
You never know when that moment
will become a memory,
So, excuse me while I savor every moment
While living in it.

Grief: Process of Healing

What is denial?

Denial is the moment you hear the news and refuse to believe it. Denial is your heart not accepting what's real.

It's terrifying to hear someone passed on, to explain the feeling is a loss for words. It's like your heart is battling your mind, trying to comprehend how exactly you feel, because you've yet to process it. It's many mixed emotions. It's trying to understand why. We live in the moment every day; we don't think to wonder how we would feel when someone passes until it's time to face it up close.

The first step to grief is denial.

Your brain jumps directly to denial because you want your loved one well and here. You start to feel guilty about the things you didn't do to help.
You suddenly blame yourself.
You wonder what could have been.
Why it happened, was there a bigger purpose?

You become numb during the denial moment.

Grief: Process of Healing

What is the difference between grief and mourning?

Grief is your internal speaking; it's how you feel. That rush of loneliness, loss, and hopelessness you feel. You find yourself wanting to be alone because the temporary high bliss of others is scary when coming down. Sometimes, you find yourself not eating, sleeping, or anything that's in your daily routine. Depression takes over, a scary rush of emotions you will feel. It's important to feel them all. Accept them. Don't let them take you over, your loved one wouldn't want you hurting yourself over their loss.

Mourning is the actions we take. Whether you choose to change your daily routine to let the loss and grieving become of you. When you go to a funeral you wear black clothes, but why? Change your way of thinking. Wear something vibrant, don't add to your grief by feeding into it. The longer you do, the longer you will mourn. Activities you usually like are out the window during mourning. You have no interest for anything or anyone.

Grief heals, but the aftermath lasts a lifetime. Mourning can last however long you decide to soak in it.

Grief: Process of Healing

"Will I ever be the same"

The answer is no. The death of a loved one leaves a mark on you that is forever imprinted in your heart and mind. It's something unforgettable. It's lifechanging. You need to adapt to a whole new world without them. It breaks you, overall, it changes you. You start to wonder if you will ever go back to who you were before you lost them, unfortunately you won't. In any situation, you never go back, only forward. You grow through every situation you go through. Time heals all wounds and your healing journey is however long it takes you to overcome the loss. It will always stick with you; you will always remember the feeling. Events will come around to make you remember, or the simple signs that keep them in your daily routine.

Admire the gestures your angels come around to give you, that's their soul alive.

Grief: Process of Healing

Am I ill? Do I need therapy?

When I lost my friend, I fell into a deep depression. I lost sight of myself and everything around me. When I was around loved ones, they gave me the feeling I needed to stay afloat but when we departed, I fell deeper into my confused depression. I never felt something so strong and hurtful, it was something I couldn't explain at the time. I would cry and talk to God mostly.

I reached out and got a therapist for the first time. It was different, I wasn't a fan of going to therapy, maybe I didn't have the right fit. I don't shame therapy, everyone heals differently. Therapy isn't for me. I reached out because I accepted, I was depressed, and I thought I needed help. I was confused and lost, which caused my depression.

Grief: Process of Healing

I realized the way to heal was to feel even though it was painful. I made it a mission to understand death and stopped trying to understand why our loved ones are taken so soon but accept them in spirit. It's heartbroken till this day, I'm a mess sometimes.

You aren't ill because you're grieving over a loved one. You are going though a rage of emotions you haven't felt before and it can scare you to believe you're ill.

I advise to do what you believe is best for your healing process. If feeling everything is entirely too much for you, seek therapy.

Don't ever believe you're ill because you love someone so much, you can't understand how it's possible to love and let them go.

Grief: Process of Healing

"Don't settle,
It's important to always give your soul
Exactly what it needs,
To fulfill you.
Remember,
Just because you love someone
Doesn't mean you will forever.
Sometimes there's pain,
You part ways
And you grieve the loss."

Grief: Process of Healing

We need to understand,
We can't be selfish when it comes to death.

To understand,
Everyone's road comes to an end,
But we still love them.
They're just not in human form
But they're near.

Grief: Process of Healing

"Every day is another day to keep going,
The hurt you feel may last awhile
But the longer you dwell in the pain
And the loss,
The longer it will hurt.

Everyone experiences pain in different ways,
Because we all feel differently,
One thing for sure,
We all heal,
We all make it through.

It's up to you to let yourself.

Grief: Process of Healing

It's brutal,
To accept the fact your loved one
Will no longer be here physically.
You spend forever grieving,
You never truly get over the loss
Of someone who truly has a place in your heart.

Grief: Process of Healing

I never made it passed the storm,
I always lived it
Until I overcame it.
I watched it almost kill me
Until I finally took control.

Death
Losing loved ones
Outgrowing
Letting go
Change

These have been my biggest challenges
I fear facing,
I feared feeling
I feared what would come next.
Fear burdened me
Until I found peace in pain,
Until I found myself in the storm.

What I feared no longer consumed me,
I took control.

Grief: Process of Healing

Death

It's the scariest thing in the world, to know the ones you love will one day leave this earth. Their spirit will fly into another world but will still follow us and keep us safe. We choose to be selfish and ask for them to still be here, without understanding they're still living on. They're closer to us than before. Guilt becomes one of the biggest feelings, as we said things we can't take back. That's why it's important to always say you love someone. Hold no regrets, life's too short. I lost many to God. I cried tears until I had none left. I was confused how it could be possible to live without them. My heart couldn't rest without their love. I wondered how it was possible to live on without them being whole. I was selfish when it came to want them to be around forever. Whether I knew it was coming or it was unexpected, I couldn't grasp the concept of never seeing them again. It didn't make sense until God made it. I learned to accept death as a part of life even though it scared me. even after death, there's life.

Souls don't die, bodies do.
The spirit that lives on, is what should be focused on, that's the love we know.

Grief: Process of Healing

Goodbyes didn't always mean
Losing someone I couldn't get back, from death,
I realized any goodbye hurts.
Especially from afar,
Knowing they're out there in the world
And having to separate that love
From the soul that crossed my path
Once upon a time,
Because the new version of them
Isn't one I'm meant to be paired with.

I learned goodbyes don't always hold pain,
Instead,
Bring closure,
A new sense of purpose.

Moving on,
Didn't bring that heart aching pain I once knew.

Goodbyes brough peace,
The kind of peace
Being with them couldn't give me.

Grief: Process of Healing

Write a letter to your angel

Grief: Process of Healing

Write a letter to someone you outgrew

Grief: Process of Healing

What is your grieving process?

Grief: Process of Healing

Grief: Process of Healing

I hope this collection made you feel something, even if it didn't touch you in the ways you thought it would, or you haven't yet felt this pain. I pray you never need to. This topic is a hard one to put into exact words, but I did the best I could with the experiences I've had.
Overall,
I hope you enjoyed the read.
To the ones who needed it the most,
I'm praying for your healing.

Book pictures are appreciated,
Highly recommended!

If you enjoyed,
Feel free to leave a review on Amazon or
Goodreads. Love to hear your feedback.

For more of my work:

Email: moonsoulchild@outlook.com
Instagram: @moonsoulchild
Twitter @moonssoulchild
Facebook @moonsoulchild

Printed in Great Britain
by Amazon